Risk Management based on

Other publications by Van Haren Publishing on IT-management

Van Haren Publishing specialises in publications on Best Practices, methods and standards within IT-management and management. These publications are grouped in two series: *ITSM Library* (on behalf of ITSMF Netherlands) and *Best Practice*. At the publishing date of this publication the following books are available:

ITIL:

Foundations of IT Service Management based on ITIL, (English and and in 4 translations; also as a cd-rom)
IT Service Management based on ITIL (German, French, Japanese, Russian, Spanish)
IT Service Management - een samenvatting, 2de druk, a pocket guide (Dutch)
IT Service Management - een leerboek (Dutch)

ISO/IEC 20000:

ISO/IEC 20000 - a pocket guide (English)

ISO 27001 and ISO 17799

Information Security based on ISO 27001 and ISO 17799 - a management guide (English)
Implementing Information Security based on ISO 27001 and ISO 17799 - a management guide (English)

CobiT:

IT Governance based on CobiT - a pocket guide (English, German)

IT Service CMM:

IT Service CMM - a pocket guide (English)

ASL:

ASL - a Framework for Application Management (English)
ASL - Application Services Library - a management guide (English, Dutch)

BiSL:

BiSL - a Framework for Business Management and Information management (Dutch; English edition Summer 2006)
BiSL - Business information Services Library - a management guide (Dutch; English edition Autumn 2006)

ISPL:

IT Services Procurement op basis van ISPL (Dutch)
IT Services Procurement based on ISPL - a pocket guide (English)

PRINCE2:

Project management based on PRINCE2- Edition 2005 (Dutch, English , German, due Spring 2006)

MSP:

Programme management based on MSP (Dutch, English)
Programme management based on MSP - a management guide (English)

MoR:

Risk management based on MoR - a management guide (English)

Topics & Management instruments

Metrics for IT Service Management (English)
Six Sigma for IT Management (English)

MOF/MSF:

MOF - Microsoft Operations Framework, a pocket guide (Dutch , English, French, German, Japanese)
MSF - Microsoft Solutions Framework, a pocket guide (English, German)

For a recent update on the VHP publications, see our website: www.vanharen.net.

Risk Management based on M_o_R®
A Management Guide

Van Haren
PUBLISHING

Colophon

Title: Risk Management based on M_o_R® - A Management Guide

Author: Jane Chittenden (Lead)

Chief Editor: Jan van Bon

Publisher: Van Haren Publishing, Zaltbommel, www.vanharen.net

ISBN: 90 77212 68 X

Print: First edition, first impression, May 2006

Layout and design: DTPresto design and layout, Zeewolde - NL

Copyright: Van Haren Publishing 2006

Printer: Wilco, Amersfoort - NL

For any further enquiries about Van Haren Publishing, please send an e-mail to: info@vanharen.net

Aknowledgements

The Author and Chief Editor gratefully thank and acknowledge the following for their assistance in the production of this title:

Rubina Faber	Regal Training
Charles Fox	Core i.s.
Martyn Clements	HMRC
Tom Abram	Mantix
John Humphries	The Service Station
Andrew Pitkeathly	HMG Land Registry

We are also extremely grateful to the Best Practice User Group for use of their facilities for the QA of this title.

Best Practice User Group™ is the leading support organization for users of the OGC Best Practice products, such as PRINCE2™, Managing Successful Programmes and Management of Risk. BPUG organize workshops and conferences, represent users on technical and examination boards and host the official Issues Log on our web site.
For more information please see www.usergroup.org.uk.

Contents

1 Introduction

1.1 About this book

This book provides a quick reference to risk management in a handy pocket sized format.

The information in this pocketbook is based primarily on Management of Risk (*M_o_R*, the best practice approach developed and owned by the OGC, the UK Office of Government Commerce). The pocketbook includes other sources of best practice advice on risk management published by OGC. The principles, processes and key terms described in this pocketbook are consistent with OGC's advice and guidance on risk management.

1.2 What is risk management?

In this guide risk is defined as uncertainty of outcome, whether positive opportunity or negative threat.

Risk management is the process of identifying and controlling the organisation's exposure to risk. This process should be consistently applied across all sections of the organisation (and partners, where applicable); it should be cost effective and proportionate to the risks being managed.

The first phase of risk management is concerned with identifying and assessing the risks relating to planned activities, then making informed choices about taking risks (risk analysis). The second phase is about ongoing management of risks – that is, subsequently controlling those risks. It requires access to reliable and up to date information about risks and a decision making framework that is understood by all involved.

Table 1.1 shows the key terms used in risk management.

Key term	Explanation
Risk management framework	Sets the context within which risks are managed - how they will be identified, assessed, controlled, monitored and reviewed
Risk identification	Process of listing and describing sources of risks, threats, events and consequences
Risk assessment (also known as risk evaluation)	Assessment of the probability and impact of an individual risk
Risk management strategy	The strategy for managing a related set of risks for a specific programme, project or operational service
Risk register	Document that is used to capture and maintain up to date information about all the identified risks for a specific programme, project or operational service
Risk owner	Role, or individual, with authority to manage the risk and ensure it is controlled
Risk allocation	Process of determining the party best placed to manage a specific risk

Table 1.1 *Key risk management terms*

See Appendix A for a glossary of risk management terms; see Appendix B for outlines of risk documents.

1.3   Risk, threat or issue?

Risks, threats and issues are often confused. Risks should always be considered in relation to objectives; so, for example, the objective is to provide a new hospital. There is a **risk** of late delivery – a negative outcome. Conversely, there is a **risk** (a positive opportunity) that the building will be finished ahead of schedule.

A **threat** is a factor that could lead to a risk occurring – that is, it will be the cause of a risk. For example, there is a general threat of severe weather, which could disrupt the building schedule. If that threat becomes reality, there is a consequent risk of time and cost overruns.

An **issue** is a concern that cannot be avoided. It may be:

* a risk that has materialised and needs to be managed
* a required change to programmes/projects/operational services
* a problem affecting a programme/projects/operational services.

CHAPTER 2

Risk management in context

2.1 Overview

There are three perspectives on risk management, depending on your role and responsibilities in your organisation.

If you are a senior manager, especially a member of the organisation's management board, **corporate governance** will be an important priority for you. Corporate governance is concerned with accountability for the organisation's actions, for which it must demonstrate proper practice, procedures and records.

If you are involved in strategic planning, you will be making deliberate choices about **risk and innovation** in order to exploit opportunities to do new things or to do things in new ways. Your organisation's willingness to 'take a risk' will influence your decisions in this area; this is often referred to as 'risk appetite'.

If you are involved in programme and project delivery or operational services, choices have already been made about a particular course of action and the associated risks. Your task will be to focus on **managing the delivery risks** that have already been identified, together with continually scanning for emerging risks as they develop and managing those as well. *OGC's Management of Risk (M_o_R)* guidance is primarily concerned with this perspective.

2.2 Corporate governance

Corporate governance is concerned with how companies should be run, in the context of society as well as the law and best practice. It also applies to not-for-profit organisations. It is often described as a framework of accountability to customers, stakeholders and the wider community within which an organisation takes decisions to achieve its objectives. OGC defines corporate governance as *the ongoing activity of maintaining a sound system of internal control to safeguard investment and the organisation's assets.*

"Corporate Governance is concerned with holding the balance between economic and social goals and between individual and communal goals. The corporate governance framework is there to encourage the efficient use of resources and equally to require accountability for the stewardship of those resources. The aim is to align as nearly as possible the interests of individuals, corporations and society." (Sir Adrian Cadbury in 'Global Corporate Governance Forum', World Bank, 2000)

In the UK, fully listed companies must comply with the revised Combined Code on Corporate Governance, which was issued by the Financial Reporting Council in July 2003. Other companies may choose to adopt it on a voluntary basis. The main consideration in risk management is that there must be an annual report to discuss internal controls and risk management. In Europe, there are similar corporate governance codes which may affect the way companies are directed and controlled within the European Union.

In the United States, Sarbanes-Oxley legislation was passed in 2002 to strengthen corporate governance and restore investor confidence, in response to a number of major corporate and accounting scandals.

For the banking sector worldwide, the Basle II Capital Accord was developed by the banking regulators from the G-10 countries. This Accord, released in 2004, requires all internationally active banks to adopt similar or consistent risk management practices for tracking and reporting exposure to operational, credit and market risks. Compliance is not yet required, but most financial institutions are working towards compliance.

When working well, an organisation's corporate governance provides clear direction, anticipates threats, communicates with interested parties and takes appropriate action. Poorly governed organisations do not know where risks can occur or have occurred; they do not scan their business environment or listen to their stakeholders.

2.3 Risk and innovation

Innovation is important for commercial success, staying ahead of the competition and winning new markets. But it is just as important for not-for-profit organisations – for solving apparently intractable policy problems or finding better ways of delivering services.

Innovation brings its own risks because of doing things differently or doing things that have never been done before. Successful private sector companies take these risks deliberately and manage them well. Public sector organisations find this more difficult; they are traditionally risk averse, perhaps because risk taking is associated with the possibility of something going wrong.

Decisions about innovation and risk are made when formulating strategy and strategic planning. These decisions are primarily concerned with long-term goals; these set the context for decisions at other levels of the organisation.

Innovation will mean change, which is inherently risky. Big bang implementation is especially risky. This is when a major project involves one or more of the following:
- no way back to a more stable environment because it is a completely new service or because it is impossible/too expensive to revert to the previous way of working
- all or most of the requirements/functions/functionality are delivered in one single step from contract award to implementation (rather than as modules), with no interim check points such as interim progress reviews
- the project is delivered to all or most of the customers in one step (rather than incrementally) by customer group/segment, by volume, by geographical area
- all or most of the benefits of the investment in business change are dependent on completion of the project, with no significant benefits delivered at intermediate steps.

'Big bang' implementation must be avoided unless there is a compelling reason to do so, such as a genuine national emergency. Where there has to be 'big bang' implementation, it must be supported by an appropriate plan that demonstrates exactly how the risks will be managed and it must be subjected to intense scrutiny.

The box below summarises high risk factors in major change.

High risk factors

Complexity – a number of complex elements, high degree of interdependency with other projects and/or technology innovation

Uncertainty - about whether the proposed solution to a problem will work and/or where the requirement is unclear and/or the end-user needs will be met

Scale – large numbers of people involved and/or multiple customer groups and/or wide geographical spread affected by the project

Sensitivity – likelihood of embarrassment for the organisation if the project fails

Multiple partners/delivery agents

2.4 Managing risks to delivery

Figure 2.1 shows four levels at which risk is managed. The **strategic** level is outlined above, where choices are made about risk, in relation to innovation and plans for delivering the business strategy. The other three levels are concerned with actual delivery of the organisation's strategy.

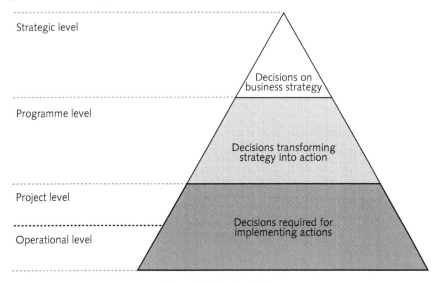

Figure 2.1 *Levels of risk*

At the **programme** and **project** levels the focus is on medium-term goals, to deliver the organisation's strategic objectives.

Programme and project managers have to juggle things from top level to the bottom; they advise on the choices that are made about risk.

At any time during the programme's life, there may be circumstances or situations that could have a detrimental impact on the programme. Such circumstances or situations are the risks and issues that the programme must manage and resolve.

As part of the toolkit for dealing with issues at project level, managers will need a programme risk policy or a strategic level risk policy to give overall guidance and direction on how risk should be managed.

At the **operational** level the emphasis is on short-term goals to ensure ongoing continuity of business services.

See Chapters 7, 8, 9 and 10 for detailed advice on managing risk at each level.

CHAPTER 3

What is at risk and why

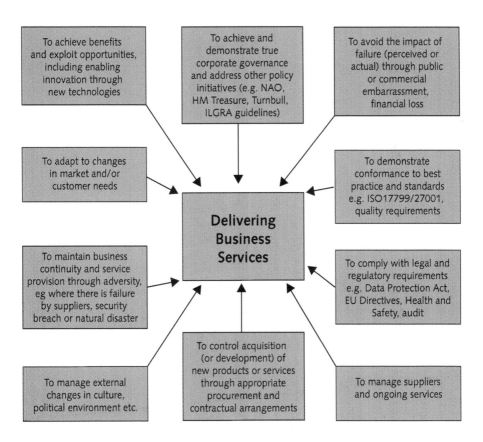

Figure 3.1 *Areas where risk needs to be managed*

3.1 Introduction

Risks to the business can come from a wide range of sources. Figure 3.1 shows the areas where most organisations can expect to encounter risk and hence why they need to have risk management processes in place. There are many ways to categorise risk. The categories below can be used as a starting point for identifying your organisation's main areas of risk:

- strategic/commercial risks
- economic/financial/market risks
- legal and regulatory risks
- organisational management/human factors
- political/societal factors
- environmental factors/Acts of God (force majeure)
- technical/operational/infrastructure risks.

Appendix C investigates different categories of risk in more detail.

3.2 Where risks occur

As shown in Figure 2.1, there are risks at the strategic level, concerned with setting and maintaining strategic direction and business objectives. They can occur at a programme level, where interdependencies between projects and the wider business environment are being managed. At the project level the risks typically relate to progress against plans; at the operational level they may relate to technical problems, supplier management or the wider services marketplace.

You should be aware that risks can move from one level to another. A straightforward technical risk, for example, might become a serious reputational risk because customers lose confidence. This highlights the need to understand the scope of decisions at the different levels and ensure that relevant information about risks is shared throughout the organisation.

You also need to be aware of the interdependencies of risks and how they can affect each other. For example, stakeholders changing the project scope at the same time as insisting on bringing the delivery date forward is a common example of risk compounding. Interdependencies can occur at all levels and across different levels. They often cross boundaries, such as ownership, funding, decision making, organisational or geographical boundaries. You must be able to assess risk and communicate across these boundaries.

Level	Typical risks at this level
Strategic/corporate	Commercial, reputational, financial, political, environmental, directional, cultural, acquisition and quality risks. Information on programme, project and operational risks should be communicated to this level where they could affect strategic objectives.
Programme	Procurement/acquisition, funding, organisational, projects, security, safety, quality and business continuity risks. Information on strategic risks should be communicated to this level where they could affect programme objectives.
Project	Personnel, technical, cost, schedule, resource, operational support, quality and provider failure. Operational issues/risks should be considered at this level as they affect the project and how it needs to be run. Information on strategic and programme related risks should be communicated to this level where they could affect project objectives.
Operations	Personnel, technical, cost, schedule, resource, operational support, quality, provider failure, environmental and infrastructure failure. All the higher levels have input to this level; specific concerns include business continuity management/contingency planning, support for business processes and customer relations.

Table 3.1 *Risk related to organisational levels*

CHAPTER 4

A risk management framework

4.1　A framework for managing risk

A framework for management of risk sets the context in which risks will be identified, assessed, controlled, monitored and reviewed. It must be seamlessly integrated with everyday management and operational practices. It sets out the 'rules' for:
* identifying risks
* assessing their probability and potential impact
* quantifying risks (not necessarily financially, although this is important)
* deciding how to deal with risks
* making decisions on risk management, such as further risk reduction
* implementing decisions about risks
* evaluating how effectively risks are managed
* communication about risks
* engaging stakeholders throughout the process.

4.2　Defining a framework for management of risk

The minimum requirements for a framework for managing risk are:
* establishment of the risk policy
* identification, and when appropriate, assignment of risk owners from among the stakeholders
* definition and adoption of suitable approaches for identifying risks; assessing risks and reporting them; action to deal with risks
* definition of responsibilities for managing risk and reporting to senior management, especially risks that cross core business activities and organisational boundaries
* establishment of quality assurance (QA) arrangements to ensure that risk management reflects current good practice.

4.3   Policy on risk management

A risk management policy should:
- define the roles (and, if possible, named individuals) who are responsible for risk management
- set the criteria for when to refer decision making about risk upwards
- ensure that there are adequate processes in place to identify and manage risk
- specify how risk management processes will be monitored (including reports to the management board, at least annually)
- provide internal control mechanisms for independent audit of the risk management processes.

4.4   Who is involved

In principle, everyone in the organisation should be involved in the management of risk. In practice, there will be roles and individuals at each level of the organisation with clearly defined responsibilities for managing risk.

The management board is responsible for corporate governance, which includes assurance that risks are being managed adequately.

At the strategic level, senior service heads and strategic planners will make choices about risk; they will appraise different options for meeting business objectives by making trade-offs about the mix of cost, benefit and risk. Depending on the nature of the business, a senior individual might be responsible for risk at the corporate level.

At the programme level, the programme manager is responsible for managing risk and coordinating risk reporting from the programme's projects. In major programmes there is usually a dedicated risk manager providing specialist support.

Project managers are responsible for managing the risks relating to their own projects.

Service and contract managers are responsible for managing operational risks.

Note that partners, including suppliers, will also be involved in managing risks at the programme, project and operational level.

> **Critical success factors for management of risk**
>
> The key elements that need to be in place if risk management is to be effective, and innovation encouraged, include:
> - named individuals at senior management level to take the lead on risk management
> - risk management policies and their benefits clearly communicated to programme and project teams and to staff managing operational services
> - a framework for management of risk that is clearly understood and repeatable
> - an organisational culture that encourages well informed risk taking and innovation, with 'no-blame'
> - management of risk integrated with everyday management processes and consistently applied
> - management of risk closely linked to achievement of objectives
> - risks associated with working with other organisations assessed and managed
> - risks actively monitored, regularly reviewed and promptly acted upon.

4.5 Budgets

The cost of managing risk will depend upon the technical, political and organisational complexity involved, but it needs to be recognised, with budgets agreed and allocated. Elements to be costed include:
- development, maintenance and dissemination of the risk policy
- creation and maintenance of the supporting infrastructure for use across the organisation (including the acquisition of support tools)
- development and/or acquisition of relevant skills (including training)
- loss of business capability while implementing new processes to manage risk.

When planning projects and programmes expect to spend around 3% of your budget on an initial risk analysis and management effort, and an additional 2% on updating this throughout the development lifecycle. See Chapter 12 for a description of risk allowances for construction projects, a principle that is often adopted in other types of project.
Operational units need to develop and maintain a number of plans relating to ensuring service continuity. Major elements include information security, contingency and business continuity planning. Operational units should expect to set aside 10–30% of their budget for risk management.

CHAPTER 5

How risks are managed

5.1 Risk management overview

Risk management involves:
- processes to track the current status of risks
- timely and accurate reporting on risks
- taking prompt action to mitigate risks
- follow up to check that these actions have been effective.

Figure 5.1 shows risk management in overview.

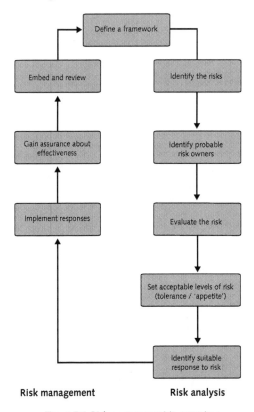

Figure 5.1 *Risk management in overview*

5.2 The Risk Management Strategy

The Risk Management Strategy is a document setting the context in which a set of risks relating to a programme, project or operational service will be identified, allocated to owners, analysed, acted upon, monitored and reviewed.
It defines processes for:
- identifying and quantifying risks
- assessing the likelihood of their occurring (probability) and impact
- ownership of individual risks
- making decisions about risk
- reviewing for effectiveness
- engaging with stakeholders on risk aspects
- contingency planning, where required.

5.3 Risk identification

Risk identification means establishing exactly what is at risk - for example, agreed activities cannot be completed within the planned timeframe or budgets are at risk of being overrun. Risks are identified early in programmes, when choices are being made about the optimum balance of cost, benefit and risk. Trade-offs are made between:
- cost - how affordable?
- benefit - how valuable/useful would this be in meeting business objectives?
- risk - how complex/uncertain/ambitious in scale?

Risk identification is a continuous process. Risks should be documented in the Risk Register for the programme, project or operational service. This captures and cooordinates information about relevant risks provides the basis for prioritisation, action, control and reporting. The Risk Register must be continually updated and reviewed throughout the life of a programme, project or operational service - this includes the operational life of a building or facility until its disposal. (See Appendix B for an outline of a Risk Register.)

The main levels of risk are:
- strategic - typically, external factors that could force a change in strategic direction
- programme level - where assumptions or interdependencies between projects change, putting benefits realisation at risk
- project level - typically time and cost overruns
- operational risks - often at the point of handover to new ways of working.

5.4   Risk ownership and allocation

Individual programme, project or service managers are responsible for ensuring that all risks are owned at the appropriate level. Each identified risk should be allocated to the individual who is best placed to deal with it - for example, a supplier or a manager in the affected business unit.

Decisions about risk allocation are discussed in detail in the next chapter, Chapter 6.

5.5   Risk assessment

Risk assessment (also known as risk evaluation) means assessing the probability of the risk occurring and the potential impact if it occurs. From an organisational perspective, it is important to consider the total level of risk as well as individual risks, to check whether an unacceptable level of risk has been reached overall.
Risk assessment should take into account any interdependencies or other factors outside the immediate scope under investigation:
- **probability** is the evaluated likelihood of a particular threat or event actually happening, including a consideration of the frequency with which this may arise
- **impact** is the evaluated effect or result of a particular risk actually happening.

Some types of risk, such as financial risk, can be evaluated in numerical terms. Others, such as adverse publicity, can only be evaluated in subjective ways. You should develop a framework for categorising risks, as (say) very high, high, medium, low, very low.

Probability criteria could be defined as:
- very low: 0-5% (extremely unlikely, or virtually impossible)
- low: 6-20% (low but not impossible)
- medium: 21-35% (fairly likely to occur)
- high: 36%-80% (more likely to occur than not)
- very high: more than 80% (almost certainly will occur)

Figure 5.2 shows a grid comparing the probability of occurrence to impact in terms of the number of risks. Qualitative words or quantitative data may be used to label the axes.

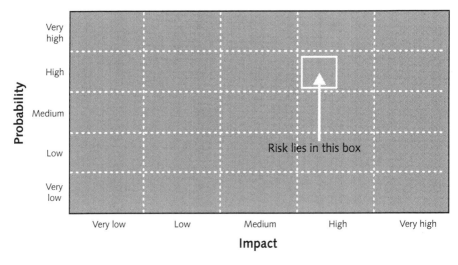

Figure 5.2 *Probability and impact matrix*

There are many ways in which risks can be assessed - see Appendix D: Techniques.

5.6   Responses to risk

These can be summarised as 'the four Ts':

- **transfer** the risk to the party best placed to manage it
- **tolerate** the risk -the 'do nothing' option, which means the programme / project / service will accept the consequences of the risk happening.
- **terminate** the risk by rescoping to remove the risk
- **treat** the risk by taking corrective actions to reduce the probability or impact of the risk.

Some risk is unavoidable and cannot be managed to a tolerable level - for example, many organisations have to accept the risk of terrorist events that are outside their control. Contingency plans are needed for these situations.

5.7   Implementing actions and reporting on risk

There will be a cost implication in managing risk - for example, allowing for a longer development time for a new IT system. The costs should be accounted for separately from the main programme or project budget (see Chapter 12 for a description of a risk allowance). Risk actions should be planned, resourced and implemented. Stakeholders should be kept informed, especially if they are directly affected.

Reporting on risks at the programme level includes information from the projects that make up the programme. There is monthly reporting (or as required) coordinated by the Programme Office. A useful way to show the aggregated risk situation is to allocate status to risks as Red (must take immediate action); Amber (proceed with caution) and Green (progressing without problems) and then to plot the position of these risks on a matrix that indicates their strategic importance. At a glance, senior managers can then see whether the overall exposure to risk is becoming unacceptable.

The same principles should be applied for operational services.

5.8 Assurance and effectiveness of risk management

For individual programmes, projects and operational services there should be an internal assurance process in place. Risk management processes should be assessed to determine how well risks have been managed, whether the key risks have actually been identified and how effectively they were treated.

5.9 Embedding and review organisation-wide

There should be regular reviews organisation-wide to assess how well risks are being managed overall. All aspects of the risk management process should be reviewed at least once a year to:
* analyse the effectiveness of the current process
* identify opportunities for improvement.

The *Risk Management Assessment Framework tool* developed by the UK's HM Treasury helps to evaluate the maturity of an organisation's approach to risk management (www. hm-treasury.gov.uk).

CHAPTER 6

Allocating risks

6.1 Introduction

This chapter supplements the guidance in M_o_R. It outlines the principles of risk allocation, which is the process of apportioning individual risks relating to projects and service delivery to appropriate parties. The key principle in allocating risks is to place them with the party best able to manage them. Risks are allocated across the supply chain – that is, between the organisation, its customers, its partners, its suppliers and their sub-contractors; for simplicity, this chapter assumes a customer organisation-supplier organisation relationship.

A risk is described as 'transferred' when the customer organisation decides not to manage that particular risk itself. The main advantage of transferring risk is that it can provide incentives for suppliers to deliver cost-effective services; this is a key feature of long-term service contracts.

When making decisions about risk allocation, the risks occur in three areas:
- business risk, which the customer organisation must retain – responsibility for these risks cannot be transferred to other parties. These risks occur at the strategic level
- service risks, which the organisation is seeking to place with the party best able to manage and control them. Some elements of individual risks will be retained by the organisation and others will be transferred to third parties. These risks occur at the programme, project and operational service levels
- supplier marketplace risks, which relate to the ability of the market sector to offer a price that offers value for money. These risks will be identified during the negotiation stage of a procurement. They also occur at the programme, project and operational service levels.

6.2 Business risks

Business risks relate to the business requirement:
- achieving business objectives
- continuing need for the service
- changes in business direction.

Jltimate business risk cannot be allocated to a supplier because if they fail to deliver what is required, the organisation remains responsible for delivering the service and for contingency plans in the event of risks materialising.

The organisation can allocate a contractual risk, but not the components that relate to its reputation, political, environmental and consequential financial risks. For public sector bodies, there are also risks relating to the government environment – policy, legislation and regulatory issues.

In addition, the organisation may be unknowingly exposed to risk that is not being managed at all. Often the inadequacy of the business case is the major source of risk, because the requirement and its implications have not been thought through. This means that the organisation does not fully understand the risks relating to its project or operational service and cannot make a realistic assessment about how its risks should be allocated.

6.3 Service risks

Suppliers can take responsibility for design, development and operational service delivery phases. Where the requirement is for organisational change, this may be outside the control of suppliers; extra care needs to be taken by the organisation to determine how best to allocate risks relating to complexity and uncertainty.

In construction projects, the procurement strategy will determine how much risk is transferred during the design and build stages.

Most **availability** and **performance risks** can be transferred. The supplier takes on the risk of absorbing the cost and resourcing consequences of making the service available when required, to the agreed levels of performance. Incentive mechanisms can be developed that reward the supplier in return for performance gains.

Service continuity risk is the acceptance of responsibility for uninterrupted delivery of the service. Some elements are usually assumed by the supplier (technical maintenance, fault fixing and continuity arrangements). Other elements may be unpredictable, such as changes in government regulation; or they may be beyond the supplier's complete control (such as power failure) and may attract a high premium.

Revenue risks relate to volume (in terms of usage) and residual value. **Volume risk** (fluctuations in service use), can be transferred by relating payment to the amount of use made of a service such as a contact centre, the number of users of a service (such as drivers using a road bridge) or the number of transactions. In each case, it is important to identify where the benefits of relating payments to usage are most likely to be realised. Certain levels of volume may have to be guaranteed so that the financial risk is reduced to a level that the supplier can manage. The customer organisation retains some of the business risk of flexibility. Payments can also be related more closely to availability/ performance criteria.

Residual value risk is concerned with the residual value of assets previously used to deliver the service, which will be realised by the supplier who takes on or retains possession of buildings, IT and other assets. The customer organisation will want to develop mechanisms for reduction in price or increased flexibility over the life of the contract to reflect the residual value that will accrue to the supplier.

Suppliers may not be best placed to manage the **risk of major business change** and may potentially attach a very high price to being exposed to such risk. But they could be contracted to adapt the service to meet periodic planned changes, building the cost of this change into their agreed service price. The intention is to give incentives to suppliers to design services that are adaptable to changing business needs and to place limits on the cost of change once contracts have been signed.

Obsolescence risk is the risk that buildings or IT will be superseded by technical advances that affect the cost of service delivery. The price of transferring this risk may be beyond the control of the supplier and must be examined very carefully.

6.4 Supplier marketplace risks

A supplier will only invest in a project if the return is commensurate with the risks it undertakes in comparison to other opportunities in the marketplace. The customer organisation can reduce the risk of lack of supplier interest by allowing scope for innovation and added value wherever appropriate.

Appendix E provides a checklist of key questions to ask at each stage of risk allocation.

CHAPTER 7

Managing risks at the strategic level

7.1 Introduction

Strategic level risks are those that the organisation must retain – they cannot be transferred to others, so the organisation must manage these risks itself. They are concerned with reputation (how others perceive it, whether positive, negative or neutral); strategic direction; its relationship with its business environment and stakeholders. Risks at this level could have such a serious impact that the organisation can no longer function.

Level	Typical risks at this level
Strategic/corporate	Commercial, reputational, financial, political, environmental, directional, cultural, acquisition and quality risks. Information on programme, project and operational risks should be communicated to this level where they could affect strategic objectives.

Table 7.1 *Summary of strategic risks*

7.2 When to manage risks at the strategic level

Risks at the strategic level should be managed routinely when:
- business planning - identifying, reviewing, agreeing and setting corporate/ organisation-wide objectives and goals
- assessing and choosing options for implementation of strategic initiatives
- formulating, submitting or reviewing feasibility studies/business cases to support future strategies
- testing the underlying assumptions within the business case or proposed strategies
- initiating, approving or reviewing programmes, projects and operational activities.

There should also be risk management activity when:
- there is any indication that changes in external factors could affect the strategy, mission, objectives and goals

- there have been changes in, or potential changes customer/stakeholder involvement
- an unforeseen event has occurred that could have an impact on the corporate objectives
- making key acquisition decisions.

7.3   Who is involved in managing strategic risks

Table 7.2 summarises the roles and responsibilities of those involved in management of risk at the strategic level.

Who should own and apply the risk process	Responsibilities
Management Board	Ownership of the overall management of risk framework and process; approval of budgets to be allocated to the management of risk
Accounting Officers or equivalent; senior stake-holders	Establishing policy on risk and signing off risk strategy, including willingness to take on risk and risk tolerance levels
Business consultants, strategy planners	Application of risk process to business changes, such as in strategy, establishment of new programmes
Risk committee, audit committee	Ensuring compliance with corporate guidance on internal control
Specialist advisors, such as security/business continuity management	Ensure risks are reported to appropriate levels and responses made

Table 7.2 *Who is involved in managing strategic risks*

8 Managing risks at programme level

8.1 Introduction

Before starting any programme or project, the organisation should make a realistic appraisal of its willingness to deal with change and the risks associated with that change.

The organisation will need to ask itself a series of questions:
- is there a clear direction set out in the business strategy?
- is there ongoing alignment to the strategy?
- are roles and responsibilities understood and accepted by top management?
- is there access to the right skills and capabilities?
- is there learning from experience in managing change?
- is there a framework for managing risk?

Level	Typical risks at this level
Programme	Procurement/acquisition, funding, organisational, projects, security, safety, quality and business continuity risks. Information on strategic risks should be communicated to this level where they could affect programme objectives.

Table 8.1 *Summary of programme risks*

8.2 Where to apply risk management

Risk management at the programme level should be applied where:
- the information about risk can influence the programme most effectively
- decisions being taken at the strategic level require programme risk information
- programme objectives are, or will be, influenced by changes to strategic objectives and vice versa
- the business case for the programme or associated projects is being revised or reviewed
- there is a requirement for a programme review

- considering projects as individual elements of strategy implementation
- considering all the projects that make up a programme as representing a single entity.

Risk management at the programme level should be applied when:
- reviewing and reporting programme status with regard to corporate and programme objectives
- providing formal approval for, or reviewing projects against, programme and project objectives, goals, business case and performance
- endeavouring to engage stakeholders in the programme
- conducting programme planning or rescheduling
- key projects are failing, or have failed to meet their objectives
- starting a new acquisition lifecycle of a programme
- preparing for programme reviews
- significant changes are proposed, planned or have occurred at any of the other levels – that is, strategy, project, operations or within the external environment
- they are an integral part of the programme/project management process.

8.3   Who is involved in managing programme risks

Table 8.2 summarises the roles and responsibilities involved in risk management at the programme level.

Who should own and apply the risk process	Responsibilities
Programme sponsors	Advising on appropriate levels of risk taking; approving funding for programme and project risk management plans
Programme owner/ Programme Director	Ensuring that risks are being managed effectively; key risks managed at the right level. Balancing an acceptable level of programme risk against business opportunity and deciding level of acceptability of individual risks
Programme Manager	Establishing and assuring the effectiveness of the risk process to be used within the programme; managing risks to the programme. Ensuring that the design process, technical change control and quality assurance address risk
Programme Office	Manage and coordinate risk information; provide guidance on suitable tools and techniques. Escalation of risks to business executive, Accounting Officers, stakeholders and appropriate management boards
Programme risk specialists, e.g. security Business Change Managers Procurement Managers Contract managers Legal, regulatory advisors Business Continuity Managers	Check feasibility of technical risks through appropriate authority Advise and provide guidance to projects on project risk within the context of the programme and relevant strategy

Table 8.2 *Who is involved in managing programme risks*

CHAPTER 9

Managing risks at project level

9.1 Introduction

Risk management at this level should be applied where:
- project objectives and goals are being assessed
- key milestones and/or decision points are reached in the project lifecycle.

It is important to adopt the guidelines set out at the programme level. Depending on the extent to which risks are being analysed and managed at corporate and programme levels, risk management at project level will either be minimal or intensive.

To start a project, information on terms of reference, scope boundary and initial plans is needed, as well as details of risk analysis that are completed at higher levels.

One of the major threats to a project is a lack of understanding of the scope of the project. This must be carefully considered, especially with regard to project definition and control.

Risk management at project level should be applied when:
- there is a change in the project lifecycle
- major acquisitions are being made as part of the project
- reassessing project benefits and the business case
- preparing to hand over from a development environment to operations
- any significant changes are notified to the project
- revisiting the cost-benefit and risk case behind the project or programme
- preparing for key milestones in the project.

Level	Typical risks at this level
Project	Personnel, technical, cost, schedule, resource, operational support, quality and provider failure. Operational issues/risks should be considered at this level as they affect the project and how it needs to be run. Information on strategic and programme related risks should be communicated to this level where they could affect project objectives.

Table 9.1 *Summary of project risks*

9.2 Who is involved in managing project risks

Table 9.2 summarises the roles and responsibilities involved in risk management at the project level.

Who should own and apply the risk process	Responsibilities
Project Board Project owner Project sponsor	Balancing an acceptable level of project risk against programme and project objectives and business opportunity. Approve funding for risk allowances
Project manager Project support office Project risk specialists	Implementing the management of risk process to be used at project level Ensuring interdependency related risks are reported and addressed
Project Delivery Managers Operations Managers	Escalation of risks to programme level and operations where required and responding to risks notified to the project
Project Work Groups/teams Business Continuity/ Security Managers	Allocation of project resources to support the risk process
Project auditors	Assessing effectiveness of risk management and providing recommendations for improvements

Table 9.2 *Who is involved in managing project risks*

CHAPTER 10

Managing risks to operational services

10.1 Introduction

Risks at the operational level include: personal risks, technical, costs, schedule, resource, operational support, quality, supplier failure, environmental issues and infrastructure failure.

If the risks are not managed, the service will be unable to deliver its business benefits and costs will increase.

Level	Typical risks at this level
Operations	Personnel, technical, cost, schedule, resource, operational support, quality, provider failure, environmental and infrastructure failure. All the higher levels have input to this level; specific concerns include business continuity management/ contingency planning, support for business processes and customer relations.

Table 10.1 *Summary of operational risks*

10.2 Where to apply risk management

Risk management at the operational level must be applied where:
- delivery of projects will impose either a major change, or potential risk, to the operational environment
- timescales for delivery put pressure on the operational environment. Serious conflicts result if the objectives of different project drivers and owners are not synchronised.
- changes in the operational environment could significantly undermine the project, programme and strategic objectives if the risks are not understood and communicated
- there is a need to identify the critical business process and technology
- changes are needed to a contract with a key supplier or service provider
- there is a need to build commitment to change
- there is a need for internal control from a corporate governance perspective
- there are regulatory and legal constraints, such as health and safety.

At the operational level, risk management should be applied when:

- considering undertaking significant commitments on behalf of the organisation
- establishing a new operational process or considering any significant change to the existing operational environment
- major investment decisions are being made
- identifying future human resource requirements for operational staff
- there is an unexpected threat to the operational environment
- anything unforeseen occurring that threatens 'business as usual'.

10.3 Who is involved in managing operational risks

Table 10.2 summarises the roles and responsibilities involved in risk management at the operational level.

Who should own and apply the risk process	Responsibilities
Directors/managers Business managers Operations managers	Balancing an acceptable level of operational risk against programme and project objectives and business opportunity; approving funding for risk management at operational level
Finance Director/Accounting Officer	Implementing the risk process to be used at the operational level
Information Security Manager Operational support staff	Ensuring interdependency related risks at the operational level are reported and addressed
Business Continuity Manager	Escalation of risks to strategic, programme and project level where required
Health and Safety Officer	Allocation of resources to support the risk management process
Facilities Manager Human Resource Managers Legal and regulatory officers Practitioners supporting the process, e.g. information security, business continuity, software engineers Auditors	Assessing effectiveness of risk management and providing recommendations for improvements

Table 10.2 *Who is involved at in managing operational risks*

CHAPTER 11

Managing risks with partners

11.1 Introduction

This chapter supplements the guidance in M_o_R. It outlines special considerations for working with partners. It extends the principles described earlier in this guide, applying them to a much more collaborative arrangement than the traditional arms-length customer-supplier relationship.

11.2 Definition of partners and partnering

In this guide **partners** are any organisation that collaborates with yours to deliver your business objectives, usually in a long-term relationship. (Legally constituted partnerships are outside the scope of this guide.) Partners may be others in the same industry sector, in another sector or suppliers. In the construction industry, for example, recommended best practice is for the client, architect, suppliers and construction team to work together as a partnering team to deliver a construction project (see the next chapter for more information about construction projects).

Partnering is a working relationship that is characterised by openness, teamwork and mutual trust. There may or may not be a contract. The relationship is often underpinned with a 'partnering code of practice'. This helps all partners understand how they will work together, including the sharing of risk.

11.3 Partnering approach to risk management

The risk management approach is similar to the approach described in Chapter 5 (How risks are managed) but takes those principles further.

Risk identification and assessment is based on a common understanding of the risks and how they will be managed. There should be common standards for assessing the probability and impact of the risks.

A **joint Risk Register** enables partners to share their assessment of risks, decisions on how the risks will be managed and subsequent reporting on risk. 'Open book' accounting helps to manage the financial aspects of risk.

Allocation of risks, as outlined in Chapter 6 (Allocating risks), places each risk with the party best able to manage the risk, but with an important difference – shared responsibility for the outcome, whoever actually manages the risk. Everyone works together to reduce risks.

Contingency planning defines what actions are taken to 'step in' by partners if risks materialise, such as service failure.

CHAPTER 12

Managing risks in construction projects

12.1 Introduction

This chapter supplements the guidance in *M_o_R*. Risk management in construction projects extends the principles outlined in Chapter 3: How risks are managed and Chapter 11: Managing risks with partners.

Construction projects have traditionally been conducted in an adversarial way, with costly delays and frequent accidents on site. Experience has shown that a partnering approach significantly reduces risk, particularly where all parties work together as an integrated project team.

12.2 Integrated project teams

This approach is recommended best practice, as described in OGC's Achieving Excellence in Construction and Constructing Excellence, the industry body that aims to deliver individual, corporate and industry excellence in construction.

An integrated project team for a construction project is made up of the client, the architect/design team, suppliers/manufacturers and the construction team. Specialist advisers to the project also join the team when required. The aim is for the team members to come together on a project basis, learning from their experience of working together and continuously improving. Where all parties to the project team are already together, they work together as described below. Where there is a procurement to obtain the services of the design and construction teams, specialist advisers will provide expertise early in the project.

12.3 Key considerations in construction projects

The **whole life** of the facility needs to be considered at the outset – that is, its design, construction, maintenance during occupancy/use and disposal at the end of its useful life. **Health and safety** aspects are important considerations. During construction the construction team must have a safe site and safe working practices; during occupancy the people using the facility need a working environment that is safe to work in and free from risks to their health; and those maintaining the facility must be able to do so efficiently without running health and safety risks.

Construction projects usually result in a facility that will last for many years – or even centuries. **Sustainability and environmental concerns** need to take account of the physical fabric of the facility, the resources it consumes and its impact on the surrounding environment from construction through to disposal.

Continuous **dialogue** between partners is essential in a construction project. Decisions about design could affect 'buildability', for example, or identify opportunities for more efficient techniques such as prefabrication and standardised components.

Late changes to design, where the implications were not thought through properly at the early stages, can have a disastrous impact on budgets and timescales. The integrated project team should be working together from the earliest stages on an 'open book' basis to identify both the risks and the opportunities.

12.4 Managing risks throughout the project lifecycle

Strategic assessment: the project lifecycle begins with an assessment of business need – whether a new facility is required (or a refurbishment) and if so, what it is intended to achieve. Risk and value management workshops are helpful in identifying stakeholder needs, strategic objectives and priorities.

Scoping: once the business need has been established, the team evaluates potential options to meet the business need and conducts a high level risk assessment.

Procurement strategy (or equivalent with existing partners): the team develops an output-based specification that describes what the facility should deliver, but not specifying in detail how that need will be met.

Finalising the business case: the client approves the statement of business need and the preferred option, including the budgetary estimate and the potential cost of the risks to the project (the risk allowance, described in more detail below). The team agrees and implements a joint risk management approach.

Outline design: the team works together to optimise the design quality and costs, including an assessment of the 'buildability' of the preferred option. Any changes to the design after this point will be high risk.

Detailed design: the team finalises the design and starts construction.

Construction: the team works together on prefabrication (as appropriate) and construction of the facility.

Readiness for service: the facility is handed over to the client for occupancy/use, following a rigorous commissioning (testing) phase.

Occupancy/use: ongoing risk management is carried out by whoever is responsible for management of the facility throughout its life, including maintenance and refurbishment as appropriate.

Disposal: decommissioning of the facility at the end of its working life, which may involve demolition or handover to another owner for a different use.

12.5 Risk responses

A risk response is decided after a risk's possible causes and effects have been considered and fully understood. One or more of the following management actions will be taken.

Risk **toleration** means that the project team accepts the consequences of a risk happening.

Risk **termination** happens when risks have such serious consequences on the project outcome that they are totally unacceptable. Measures might include a review of the project objectives and a re-appraisal of the project, perhaps leading to the replacement of the project, or its cancellation.

Risk **treatment** could achieve risk reduction (or elimination) by:

* re-design
* more detailed design or further site investigation
* different methods of construction, to avoid inherently risky construction techniques
* changing the procurement route: to allocate risk between the project participants in a different way.

Risk reduction measures lead to a more certain project outturn. They usually result in a direct increase in the base estimate and a corresponding reduction in risk allowance (see below).

Risk **transfer** to another party in the integrated project team would make a different party responsible for the consequences if the risk materialises. Risks should not be transferred until they are clearly understood. The object of transferring risk is to pass the responsibility to another party better able to manage it. A premium may be paid when a risk is transferred to another party; if so, this results in a direct increase in the base estimate and a reduction in risk allowance. Cost may not be the only criterion; it may be more efficient or effective to transfer risk. Factors that should be considered in risk transfer include:

- who is best able to control the events that may lead to the risk occurring?
- who can control the risk if it occurs?
- is it preferable for the client to be involved in the control of the risk?
- who should be responsible for a risk if it cannot be controlled?
- if the risk is transferred to a member of the integrated project team:
- is the total cost to the client likely to be reduced?
- will the integrated project team member be able to bear the full consequences if the risk occurs?
- could it lead to different risks being transferred back to the client?
- would the transfer be legally secure (will the transfer be accepted under common law)?

12.6 Risk allowances

A **risk allowance** is the amount of the project budget set aside specifically for the costs of managing risks. When estimating the cost of the project (and hence the funding required), estimates are made up in two parts – the base estimate of the costs of fees and materials etc plus an allowance for the costs of managing risks. The risk allowance is estimated on the costs of the maximum and minimum risks likely to occur; the average risk between the two extremes is then used as the basis of the risk allowance. In the early project stages, the risk allowance for each element may be greater than the base estimate. As the project develops and becomes more clearly defined, funding is spent on investigations, feasibility studies, etc. The risk allowance is steadily reduced as the risks or their consequences are minimised by good risk management and required funds are transferred to the base estimate to cover the costs of risks. At the same time the base estimate of the project will steadily increase as risks materialise.

Risk allowances should be reviewed regularly through the life of the project, and appropriate adjustments made to the base estimate and risk allowance depending on the risks materialising or not.

Variation of price due to inflation and/or currency fluctuations is a risk and should be treated in the same way as any other risk. The risk should be managed and either retained, shared, transferred or minimised as appropriate.

Appendices

A: Glossary
B: Risk documentation
C: Categorising risk
D: Techniques
E: Checklist for risk allocation

Glossary

Basle Accord II	The code of governance developed by the international banking regulatory committee
Benefits	The positive outcomes, tangible or intangible, that an activity is being undertaken to deliver, and that justify the investment
Business case	The rationale for undertaking an activity (project or programme), and for committing the necessary resources, setting out the benefits to be achieved
Business Continuity Management (BCM)	Looking at the totality of the organisation: what business services and processes are vital to ensure the business can survive into the future? This includes the derivation and integration of the planning cycle into business operations and the subsequent evaluation of any business continuity measures adopted.
Corporate governance	The overall management of an organisation where it is possible to explain/see how activities are undertaken with appropriate, associated, accountability. There is a need to establish control mechanisms and provide stewardship reports such that it is possible to see that the necessary activities are taking place.
CRAMM	A formalised security risk analysis and management methodology originally developed by CCTA (now part of the Office of Government Commerce) in collaboration with a number of private sector organisations.
ILGRA	Inter-departmental Liaison Group on Risk Assessment. Secretariat provided by the UK Health and Safety Executive (HSE)
Operational risk	Primarily those risks concerned with continuity of business services
Procurement	The whole process from identifying a business need to fulfilment of contract.
Programme	A portfolio of projects that aims to achieve a strategic goal of the organisation, planned and managed in a co-ordinated way.
Programme risk	Risk concerned with transforming high level strategy into new ways of working to deliver benefits to the organisation.
Project	A specific suite of work aiming at a unique outcome, or series of outcomes, as distinct from being a repetitive process.
Project risk	Risks that are concerned with stopping the successful completion of the project. Typically these risks include technical, cost, schedule, resource, operational support, quality and supplier issues.
Residual risk	The risk remaining after the risk response (treatment) has been applied.
Risk	Defined as uncertainty of outcome (whether positive opportunity or negative threat). It is the combination of the chance of an event and its consequences
Risk analysis	Systematic use of information to identify sources of risk and to estimate the risk and then evaluate it.

Risk evaluation	The assessment of probability and impact of an individual risk, taking into account interdependencies and other relevant factors.
Risk identification	Process to list and describe sources of risk, threats, events and consequences
Risk management	The task of ensuring that the organisation makes cost-effective use of a risk process. Risk management requires: processes in place to monitor risks; access to reliable up-to-date information about risk; the right balance of control in place to deal with those risks; decision making processes supported by a framework of risk analysis and evaluation.
Risk management framework	Sets the context within which risks are managed in terms of how they will be identified, analysed, controlled, monitored and reviewed. It must be consistent and comprehensive with processes that are embedded in management activities throughout the organisation.
Risk perception	Value or concern with which stakeholders view a particular risk
Risk process	A series of well defined steps to support better decision making through good understanding of risks and their likely impacts.
Risk owner	A role, or individual, who is in a position to manage the risk and ensure it is controlled.
Risk Register	A document used to maintain information on all the identified risks pertaining to a particular activity (project or programme).
Risk response	Actions that may be taken to bring the situation to a level where the exposure to risk is acceptable to the organisation. Individual risk responses can be to transfer (some aspects), tolerate, treat or terminate one or more risk.
Sarbanes-Oxley	Corporate governance legislation in USA with which listed companies must comply
Strategic risk	Risk concerned with where the organisation wants to go, how it plans to get there and how it can ensure survival.
Summary risk profile	A simple mechanism to increase visibility of risks. It is a graphical representation of information normally found on an existing Risk Register.

Risk documentation

B1 Business Case

Purpose: to document why the forecast effort and time will be worth the expenditure to achieve the change and anticipated benefits.

The ongoing viability of the activity can then be monitored against the business case, throughout its lifetime.

Outline of content
- Reasons for the change (business need and scope)
- Benefits and benefits realisation
- Major risks
- Costs, forecast effort and timescales
- Investment Appraisal (if appropriate).

(Business case needs to cover the strategic fit; business need and scope; possible options with associated cost and investment appraisal; notes on achievability and how this will be assessed; business model and intended approach to acquisition; and affordability.)

B2 Business Continuity Plan (BCP)

Purpose: a plan for the fast, efficient resumption of essential business operations by directing recovery actions of specified teams.

The plan deals with situations of major unforeseeable failures or disasters as well as the continuation of critical business processes. BCP will cover the whole organisation but is likely to be organised as a hierarchy based on location and/or business process such that all or part of the plan can be invoked as required to cope with the situation.

Outline of content
- General introduction and overview, covering objectives, assumptions, responsibilities, how to exercise and maintain the plan
- Plan owner
- The plan of response actions to be involved (details following (activity) plan)

- Plan invocation - details of how a significant incident is defined and is declared, damage assessment and how to trigger (or prompt) all or part of the BCP
- Communications - who should be informed, contact details and key messages (covering key stakeholders and the media). In particular this will include a list of plan holders and details of how they will receive any updates to the BCP
- Suppliers - list of any service providers and associated contracts that will be actioned in particular circumstances
- Other associated key plans and policy statements (this may include contingency plans, operational risk, security and safety guidelines).

The plan needs to cover the following information, which may be part of the above or separately documented:
- procedures for emergency situations
- fallback procedures
- follow-up procedures
- test schedules (for BCP)

Each of these will cover location, facilities, resources and essential personnel requirements.

B3   Communications Plan

Purpose: to document how information will be disseminated to, and recovered from, all stakeholders in the activity (e.g. project or programme). It identifies the means / medium and frequency of communication between the different parties. It is used to establish and manage ongoing communications concerning the activity. This is a general management product which needs to identify the activity or level it relates to (such as a specific project or the strategic level of the organisation).

Outline of content
- List of stakeholders and their information requirements
- Communication mechanisms to be used (such as written reports, seminars, workshops, videos, e-mails, newsletters)
- Key elements of information to be distributed by the different mechanisms - including frequency and information collection and collation
- Roles and responsibilities of key individuals responsible for ensuring communication is adequate/appropriate and timely

- Identification of how unexpected information from other parties (including stakeholders) will be handled within the scope of the activity.

B4 Contingency Plan

Purpose: a plan that provides an outline of decisions and measures to be adopted if defined circumstances should occur in relation to a specific activity (e.g. project or service).

Outline of content
- The plan (see (Activity) plan), plus
- Information concerning the event/incident that is the trigger (or prompt initiation) for implementation of the contingency plan
- Plan owner
- Details of distribution and storage (showing how people will get a copy of the plan so that they can take the appropriate action)
- Resource allocation may be dependent on contracts – in this case details of contracts should be included.

B5 Management of Risk Policy

Purpose: to define how management of risk will be handled within the associated context (could be organisation-wide or for a specific activity such as a project). It covers the lifetime of the activity. It provides information on roles, responsibilities, processes and procedures, standards, tools, facilities and documentation to be produced. The policy may need to be adapted for different levels of the organisation.

Outline of content
- View of how processes for management of risk are to be adopted (such that they are appropriate to the size and nature of the context)
- The benefits that management of risk will achieve (within the context)
- Roles and responsibilities for management of risk and ownership of this policy, associated processes and identified risks
- List of standards, required facilities, tools and documentation requirements
- Mechanisms for monitoring application of management of risk
- Criteria and rules for escalation of risk information.

B6   (Activity) Plans for Programme and/or Project

Purpose: A plan relates to a specific activity (e.g. project). It provides a statement of how and when the objectives of the activity are to be achieved.

It provides the business case with the planned resourcing costs and identified major control (decision) points.

Once approved, a plan acts as a reference against which progress can be monitored.

Outline of content
- Plan description: brief description of the scope of the activity planning assumptions, prerequisites and constraints
- Activity network or overall schedule information
- Information on key (outcomes and/or products) and/or benefits (dis-benefits) expected
- Budgetary information
- Table of resource requirements (requested or assigned)
- Risks and issues.

B7   Risk Register

Purpose: in relation to a specific activity or plan (e.g. project), the risk register lists all the identified risks and the results of their analysis and evaluation. Information on the status of the risk is also included.

These details can then be used to track and monitor their successful management as part of the activity to deliver the required, anticipated benefits.

Outline of content
- Risk identification number (unique within the register)
- Risk type (where indication helps in planning responses)
- Risk owner raised by (person)
- Date identified
- Date last updated
- Description
- Probability
- Impact
- Proximity
- Possible response actions
- Chosen action

- Target date
- Action owner/custodian (if differs from risk owner)
- Closure date
- Cross references to plans and associated risks and may also include
- Risk status and risk action status.

Risk ID No.	Raised By And Date	Description of the risk (Source or Threat)	Impact VL, L, M H, VH			Prob. VL, L, M, H, VH	Prob. Proximity	Action	Target Data	Owner
			Time	Costs	Quality					
1			L	L	M	VL				
2			H	H	M	M				
3			H	L	VH	H				

Figure B1 *Section from a risk register*

B8 Security Policy

Purpose: to provide a definition of security measures to be adopted for the organisation. The security policy must provide clear direction such that all employees, partners and associates can see their own role and responsibility for security. It also provides the metrics within which security measures can be assessed to ensure ongoing adequacy.

Note: further information can be found in British Standard BS7799.

Outline of content
- Objectives and scope of the policy (a single policy may all aspects of security or may be concerned with individual aspects such as physical security or information security)
- Importance and benefits (goals and management principles) for adopting this policy
- Roles and responsibilities of management, employees and other affected people
- Definition of how security incidents will be reported and handled (processes to invoke)
- Relationship to other policies and guidelines (which may include risk, business continuity, personnel and statutory requirements)

- Ownership of this policy
- Details of how often and what manner this policy is to be updated
- Details of availability (e.g. how will employees etc. be given access, and be kept up to date)

B9   Stakeholder Map

Purpose: documents all parties (individuals or groups) who have an interest in the outcome of the proposed activity. This may include individuals or groups outside the business. For each stakeholder, their interests are identified and the map is used to ensure all their interests are catered for, including keeping them informed and accepting feedback.

Outline of content
- List of stakeholders
- List of interests (issues that concern them and their attitude towards aspects of the situation which present a risk)
- Matrix of stakeholders to interest

B10 Summary Risk Profile

Purpose: a mechanism to increase visibility of risk.
It is a graphical representation of information normally found in a risk register. It is associated with a specific risk register at a particular point in time.

Outline of content
- Identification of associated Risk Register and its version/date.
- Grid showing probability against impact.
- Risk from register plotted (once effects of mitigation have been taken into account).
- Risk tolerance line (showing which risks need information escalating so that decisions can be taken/approved).

Categorising risk

There are a wide number of available prompt lists to help you to categorise risk. These should be adapted to individual circumstances. This appendix gives examples of prompt lists that can be used to help an organisation consider the areas of most concern.

C1 Strategic risk – major threats

Sources of threat that may give rise to significant strategic risks include:
- budgeting (relates to availability or allocation of resources)
- fraud or theft
- unethical dealings
- product and/or service failure (resulting in lack of support to business processes)
- public perception and reputation
- lack of business focus
- exploitation of workers and/or suppliers (availability and retention of suitable staff)
- environmental (mis)management (issues relating to fuel consumption, pollution, etc.)
- occupational health and safety mismanagement and/or liability
- failure to comply with legal and regulatory obligations; and/or contractual aspect (can you sue or be sued?)
- civil action
- failure of the infrastructure (including utility supply systems, computer networks etc.)
- failure to address economic factors (such as interest rates, inflation, exchange rates)
- political and market factors (e.g. for management of risk, security, etc.)
- operational procedures – adequate and appropriate
- information/communication – adequate and appropriate
- capability to innovate (to exploit opportunities)
- failure to control intellectual property (e.g. as a result of abuse or industrial espionage)
- failure to take account of widespread disease or illness among the workforce
- failure to complete to published deadlines or timescales
- failure to take on new technology where appropriate to achieve objectives

- failure to invest appropriately
- failure to control IT effectively
- failure to establish a positive culture following business change
- vulnerability of resources (material and people)
- failure to establish effective contingency arrangements in the event of a product and/or service failure
- failure to establish effective continuity arrangements in the event of a disaster
- inadequate insurance/contingency provision
- disasters such as fire, flood, building subsidence, bomb incident.

C2 Threats to projects or programmes

The categories below can be used as a starting point for identifying your organisation's main areas of risk in relation to projects or programmes.

Corporate/commercial risks:
- Under-performance to specification
- Management's underperformance against expectations
- Contractors go out of business
- Insolvency of financiers
- Failure of suppliers to meet contractual requirements; this could be in terms of quality, quantity, timescales or their own exposure to risk
- Insufficient capital revenues
- Market fluctuations
- Fraud/theft
- Partnerships failing to deliver the desired outcome
- The situation being non-insurable (or cost of insurance outweighs the benefit)
- Lack of availability of capital investment.

Economic/financial/market risks:
- Exchange rate fluctuation
- Interest rate instability
- Inflation
- Shortage of working capital
- Failure to meet projected revenue targets
- Market developments will adversely affect plans.

Legal and regulatory risks:
- New, or changed, legislation may invalidate assumptions upon which the activity is based
- Failure to obtain appropriate approval such as planning consent
- Unforeseen inclusion of contingent liabilities
- Loss of intellectual property rights
- Failure to achieve satisfactory contractual arrangements
- Unexpected regulatory controls or licensing requirements
- Changes in tax or tariff structure
- Infringement of personal data protection criteria.

Organisational management / human factors:
- Management incompetence
- Inadequate corporate policies
- Inadequate adoption of management practices
- Poor leadership
- Key personnel who have inadequate authority to fulfil their roles
- Poor staff selection procedures
- Lack of clarity over roles and responsibilities
- Vested interests creating conflict and compromising the overall aims
- Individual or group interests will be given unwarranted priority
- Personality clashes
- Indecision or inappropriate decision making
- Inadequate management of expectations
- Lack of operational support
- Inadequate or inaccurate information
- Health and safety compromised – for example:
  - working environment presents physical dangers
  - staff under stress for significant, sustained periods.

Political / societal factors:
- Change of government policy (national or international)
- Change of government
- War and disorder
- Adverse public opinion / media intervention.

Environmental factors / Acts of God (force majeure):
- Natural disasters
- Storms, floods, etc.

- Pollution incidents
- Transport problems, including aircraft/vehicle collisions.

Technical/operational/infrastructure risks:
- Inadequate design
- Professional negligence
- Human error/incompetence
- Infrastructure failure
- Operational lifetime shorter than expected
- Residual value of assets lower than expected
- Increased dismantling/decommissioning costs
- Safety being compromised
- Performance failure (people or equipment)
- Residual maintenance problems
- Scope creep
- Unclear expectations/objectives
- Breaches in physical security/information security
- Lack or inadequacy of business continuity and contingency measures with regard to this activity
- Unforeseen barriers or constraints due to infrastructure.

C3   Operational risks

Aspects to consider here include:
- lack of clarity of service requirements
- inadequate infrastructure to provide required operational services
- inadequate or inappropriate people available to support the required service provision
- inappropriate contract in place and/or inadequate contract management to support required level of service provision
- changing requirements, enabled in an uncontrolled way
- products passed to operational teams without due consideration to implementation, handover and subsequent maintenance, decommissioning
- unexpected or inappropriate expectations of service users
- inadequate incident handling
- lack or inadequacy of business continuity or contingency measures with regard to maintaining (critical) business services
- lack of investment in infrastructure to support future needs/opportunities
- failing to meet legal or contractual obligations.

Techniques

D1 Documentation techniques

Models can be a useful way of comparing the results of evaluation of risks at different levels. Spreadsheets can be used to provide an overview of a Summary Risk Profile.

D2 The Business Excellence Model

The Business Excellence Model provides the framework for assessment of identifying how well your organisation is performing and can be applied to all levels of an organisation. The model is made up of nine criteria split between enablers and results. It forms a scoring system for each of the nine categories.

Primarily the model will look for documentation of:
* a framework for Management of Risk
* security policy
* business continuity plans.

Thus the adoption of this model will provide an assessment of how well risk management is being implemented and may highlight areas for improvement.

D3 Cause-and-effect diagrams

Cause-and-effect diagrams, also known as fish-bone diagrams, are graphical representations of the causes of various events, which lead to one or more impacts. Each diagram may possess several start-points (A-points) and one or more end-points (B-points). Construction of the diagram may begin from an A-point and work towards a B-point or extrapolate backwards from a B-point. This is largely a matter of preference. Some people prefer to start with an impact (B-point) and work backwards to its cause. Others prefer to start with an event (A-point) and work towards an impact.

D4 Decision trees

Decision trees are graphical representations of possible events resulting from various decisions. They are particularly useful in weighing the balance between a positive and negative decision.

Construction of the decision tree usually begins from a single premise and works towards a series of possible outcomes.

For example, a decision tree might be constructed to assess the events leading to impact of a dependent project overrunning (i.e. the impact on Project B when Project A overruns). Note that it is possible to calculate separately the probability of each event occurring and express this as a percentage or factor of 1.

In this example, Project B is dependent upon the release of resources from Project A. Project A is overrunning. Depending on the outcome of possible actions relating to the termination of Project A, the probability of the resources being released can be estimated. Note the various actions available, which can influence the outcome.

D5 Expected value

The expected value approach is useful when a tangible measure of risk significance is required together with a need to prioritise risks. The approach is most effective when providing a measurement of the benefit of risk reduction gained through team consensus in a workshop as opposed to the judgement of an individual.

The approach quantifies risk by deciding what insurance premium an underwriter would demand for insuring the risk. The simplest form of calculation to use is:

$$CI \times P\% = IP$$

where CI is the estimated cost of the risk impact, P is the probability of the impact occurring and IP is the insurance premium.

D6 Critical Path Analysis (CPA) or Critical Path Method (CPM)

Critical Path Analysis (CPA) or Critical Path Method (CPM) models and associated software are useful for any form of activity planning. The CPA model represents activities using an activity-on-arrow (or activity-on-node) network diagram. This approach is used to identify those activities that are dependent on each other, such as where one activity cannot start until one or more other activities have finished. All activities have assumed deterministic duration. Some activities can take place concurrently in order to identify where slippage will impact or where it will erode some tolerance or require invitation of contingency actions.

Using Programme Evaluation and Review Technique (PERT) models allows explicit modelling of uncertainty in a CPA framework.

D7 Monte Carlo simulation

Monte Carlo simulation is the industry standard for combining probability distributions and forms the basis of most commercial software. It is also the recommended starting point for most IS/IT projects where quantitative risk analysis is required.

Distributions are combined by 'sampling experiments'. For example, a Monte Carlo approach to PERT models involves taking one sample duration for each activity and combining them using a CPA algorithm to determine the overall project duration. This is then separated to obtain a second project duration and so on until there are enough duration to enable a frequency distribution to be established.

Monte Carlo models are highly flexible, but are subject to sampling error. Sampling error can be controlled by using large samples, at considerable cost in terms of computational effort, when accurate results are necessary. Techniques to reduce sampling error may introduce a bias in the results.

D8 Scatter diagram

A scatter diagram can be created using a similar scale to that of a probability and impact grid, but showing concentrations of risk represented by groups of dots. The benefit of such a diagram is to show more visually where the concentrations of risk are greatest.

D9 Radar chart

Another diagram that has a strong visual impact is a radar chart. Figure D1 shows a typical chart used to show the risk exposure within severity bands by focus area.

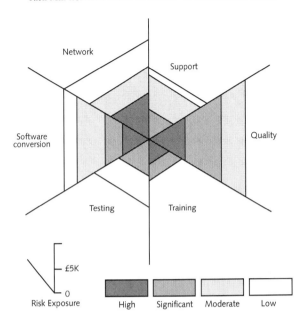

Figure D1 *Radar chart*

D10 Risk indicators

The risk indicator (sometimes termed risk factor) is the level of acceptability of a risk. Determining the risk indicator is a technique that can be used as part of the risk planning process, prior to evaluation activity.

The purpose of the risk indicator is to answer the question, Do I want to do anything about the risk? It can be set as a threshold below or above which appropriate actions may be decided. The risk indicator is thus a filter, which ensures that time is not wasted on risks that do not warrant further attention.

The risk indicator is best expressed in terms of cost, for example the cost of doing something about the risk or not, as the case may be. It may, however, be compiled as a combination of time, cost and performance factors. In practice, the business sensitivity of the programme and the commercial environment will provide the necessary information to determine the levels of acceptability.

D11 Risk identification workshops

A risk identification workshop is a group session which is designed to focus on a particular aspect of an activity for the identification of risks. The aspect may be a particular phase of a programme or the possible effects of a particular cause of risk. Participants should reflect the views of all stakeholders in the activity.

For maximum benefit, potential attendees should be asked for some basic information as input to the workshop; the workshop should be facilitated by an experienced risk practitioner, who would employ particular identification techniques and share the benefit of in-depth programme and project experience. This would lead to a broad range of risks being identified with some view of possible risk owners.

The benefit of a group session is to:
* gather the necessary fields of expertise together
* speed the process of risk identification
* reach agreement by consensus.

Risk identification workshops are most effective as half-day sessions during which, if time allows, identified risks may also be estimated and evaluated.

D12 Risk management workshops

These workshops are similar to risk identification workshops but start with a clear view of threats, which will then be considered in terms of how they can be addressed, as well as agreeing the assessment of severity of the risk. Participants should also look for any secondary risks that may be raised.

Participants should include people who may be responsible for responding to risks and/ or owning them.

Checklist: key questions to ask at each stage of risk allocation

E1 Do we understand the risks?

Have we identified all the key risks relating to this programme, project or operational service?

Have we made a thorough assessment of each one - the probability of it happening, the likely impact and cost?

Do we understand the interdependencies between risks?

How do these risks affect our key objectives?

Have we taken a long-term view, to identify possible future risks?

What is our overall exposure to risk?

E2 What can we do about risks before we decide where to allocate each one?

Have we considered the best way to deal with each risk - minimise them, mitigate them or build in contingencies?

Are there other steps we should take now - such as improving quality assurance regimes?

E3 What are the options for allocating risk?

Which are the risks that we should manage ourselves? For each one: why?
- because we can control it better ourselves?
- because it is not cost-effective to allocate it to others?
- because its likely impact will not affect critical objectives?

Which are the risks that others should manage for us? For each one: why?
- because they are better placed to influence the outcome?

- because we can identify cost-effective payment incentives that will deliver value for money?
- because the cost to us is affordable and reflects their ability and willingness to control the risk?

E4   Negotiating risk transfer with suppliers

Can we obtain the optimum risk transfer, or balance between the benefits of transferring a risk and the cost of compensating the supplier for taking it on?

Have we negotiated with each supplier to achieve the optimum balance of risk, costs and benefits?

Are our decisions on risk allocation based on a realistic assessment of the way in which risks will be managed?

Does the entire supply chain have a shared understanding of the risks and the consequences if they materialise?

Have we validated our risk plans by obtaining proposals and indicative prices from suppliers, assessing each risk and its price, taking into account:

- the nature of the requirement - high or low risk?
- the expected length of the contract - long or short-term in which to recover the development costs?
- the likelihood of predicted service volumes being exceeded, with the opportunities for increased revenue?

E5   Have we allocated risks to the right parties in the supply chain?

Can we be sure that we have not transferred the wrong risks, leading to poor value for money and unacceptable exposure to risk?

Have we made sure that we only transferred risks that are commercial in nature, where the supplier can influence the outcome?

Where risks have been transferred, is the supplier genuinely able to manage them?

E6   Can we avoid taking back transferred risks?

Are we certain that we have not taken risk back, by:
* attempting to define a technical solution?
* attempting to define how a service should be provided?

Have we preserved our supplier's freedom to propose alternatives?
Will our supplier have the freedom to choose how to handle and minimise it?

3270306R00038

Printed in Great Britain
by Amazon.co.uk, Ltd.,
Marston Gate.